HOW TO
PARALLEL PARKING AND DRIVING MANEUVERS MADE EASY!

BY HANK WYSOCKI

COPYRIGHT © 2019 BY HANK WYSOCKI

TO LEARN MORE

WWW.DRIVEREDCOACH.COM

DISCLAIMER

practices, advertising, and all other aspects of doing business in the US, Canada, or any other jurisdiction is the sole responsibility of the reader or purchaser. Neither the author nor the publisher assumes any responsibility or liability whatsoever on the behalf of the purchaser or reader of the materials. Any perceived slight of any individual or organization is purely unintentional.

INTRODUCTION

No skill can be more frustrating and time consuming to master than the skill of parallel parking. Whether you are a new driver or simply an adult driver that never took the time to learn this important technique, this book will help. The author has over 37 years in the field of driver education and has taught thousands of new drivers how to drive a car and pass their DMV road test. You could go out and blindly practice parking for endless hours trying to find the perfect system or just consume this book and do it right the first time. "How to Drive a Car" "Parallel Parking and Driving Maneuvers Made Easy!" will present two very simple easy to use methods that will have you parking like a pro in just one lesson. Simply select the method that suits your needs, follow the easy sequential steps, and then practice, practice, practice. As an added bonus you will be taught several other important driving maneuvers that are commonplace on DMV driving road tests. Step by step procedures will be provided for perfect execution of perpendicular parking, parking on a grade, as well as two and three point turns. Diagrams and step by step instructions will be provided for all the skills as well as some very helpful tips to make the specific technique even easier.

WHY I WROTE THIS BOOK

So many new drivers fixate and panic when faced with the task of parallel parking in order to pass their driving road test. Actually, many experienced drivers will also pass up that perfect parking spot when faced with the prospects and pressures of the parallel park. The truth is no one really takes the time to actually learn the correct procedures necessary to successfully execute this simple skill. Just like throwing a football or hitting a baseball a skill must be learned and practiced. More importantly the skill should be practiced properly. Perfect practice makes permanent! A skill that is learned the wrong way the first time will create a bad habit and will take hours to correct and overcome. So why not spend five minutes and learn the correct procedures and steps from "How to Drive a Car" "Parallel Parking and Driving Maneuvers Made Easy!" Once you learn the correct steps and practice them over and over, you will never shy away from that perfect parking spot ever again. Muscle memory will take over and your confidence will continue to build. Good luck and good parking.

WHY YOU SHOULD READ THIS BOOK

Why do new drivers obsess over the skill of parallel parking? Why does the DMV choose to incorporate a parallel park in many of their road tests across the United States? The simple answer is that it is only one small part of the driving road test for new drivers seeking to obtain their license. Consequently for experienced drivers it is a skill that they may never choose to use again after they have passed their driving road test. The reality is parallel parking has become a staple on the road test because it allows the examiner to observe the student driving in reverse and handling their car in a tight space. On many states' road exams this will be the only opportunity to see the student demonstrate the critical visual habits necessary to drive in reverse and park their car along a curb. If you were to ask many certified driving instructors they would tell you that mastering the skills of steering, braking and acceleration combined with good defensive driving habits are much more important than parking your car behind another vehicle. Unfortunately parallel parking is part of the majority of state road tests and must be accomplished in order to pass the road test. By purchasing this book you have taken the important first step to becoming a parallel parking master! So let's get to work.

How this Book Is Organized

This book is organized into simple easy to read chapters. Diagrams are provided for two popular parallel parking methods. Valuable hints and tips are provided to have you parking like a pro in no time. As an added bonus perpendicular parking methods and two and three point turn techniques will also be taught. Many states also require these skills to be tested in order to obtain a driver's license.

"How to Drive a Car" Parallel Parking and Driving Maneuvers Made Easy!" large clear diagrams and simple instructions make for a "stress free" reference when heading off to your favorite practice site. They help you to replicate the steps in order to enhance muscle memory, and develop the proper skills needed to park successfully.

About the Author

Hank Wysocki has been a teacher, coach and administrator for over 37 years at the college, high school, and elementary school levels. He has taught driver education and defensive driving strategies to thousands of young students and adults throughout his career. Hank is a certified Driver Education Teacher as well as an instructor of the Insurance and Point Reduction Program as an affiliate for Driver Training Associates. He is an active advocate of parent involvement within the entire driver education process for new and beginning drivers. This book is the fourth publication in a series of educational resources designed by Hank Wysocki to help promote, and educate everyone on the strategies and techniques of defensive driving. Hank's intention is to help bridge the critical gap between parents and their teenage drivers.

If there is a private or public school driving instructor involved with your driver education be sure to reinforce the correct driving habits they teach as well as the information in this book each and every time you get behind the wheel. Also, be sure to get plenty of practice opportunities to complement these lessons. Sound, repeatable, positive habits should be molded early in the driving process. Destructive, life threatening habits are much more difficult to change later in life. Good luck and safe driving.

Want some help on learning how to drive correctly and defensively go to http://www.driveredcoach.com to get plenty of free information as well as a FREE guide to passing your road test the first time. There are also two great books available on the topic of defensive driving and how to get started on the correct way to drive. Simply go to Amazon or click on the title to download these books "Teach Your Teenager How to Drive a Car" and "Save Your Teenage Driver's Life."

TABLE OF CONTENTS

CHAPTER 1 PARALLEL PARK METHOD A

New drivers fear this skill while seasoned drivers avoid this skill. Parallel parking can be super easy when executed the proper way. With a little practice everyone can become an expert. If you are a city dweller, this skill will become invaluable. Parking spots are few and far between in most large cities, so being able to position your fifteen foot car into a twenty foot space becomes a required technique. By the same token if you are teenager just learning how to drive, there is a very big chance that this intimidating skill will be part of your driver's license road test. There are several different approaches that are taught by driver education "gurus" around the country. In this book I will present two of the most popular easy to use methods. The steps and procedures for each method, and the very simple adjustments will be presented in this book. These adjustments can be applied "on the fly" when things don't go the way you expected them to.

Realize that the average length of a vehicle is around fifteen feet, and you will need at least five additional feet of space to park your car effectively. In the first method that will be presented a more flexible approach will be applied when performing this very difficult skill. In other words a learning curve is necessary and subtle adjustments are essential to adapt to an ever changing parking environment. In the second method you will rely totally and trust the method itself in order to guide you into that tight parking spot. Many new drivers begin using the first method, and after lots of practice graduate, and move on to the second method. There are fewer steps involved with Method B and the entire procedure is performed much quicker. Adaption and adjustments are a little more difficult to apply within this method.

Let's take a closer look at Method A. In Method A there are five distinct steps. Using the whole part whole method of learning it is important to first look over all five illustrations of the method provided, and then focus on each of the steps with an emphasis on mastering each step in the five step system. The next step will be to actually perform the skill breaking it down into each these five phases. So it is recommended that the first few times you practice that you should actually stop the car in each distinct phase. As you become more proficient at the skill then it is time to roll continuously through all five phases without stopping. In a perfect world effective use of the five checkmarks provided will result in a textbook parallel parking job.

Find the Perfect Spot

Drive around your city or town look for available spaces that suit your needs. The perfect spot should be one that is about ten feet larger than your car; although once you become a parking expert you will able to navigate a much smaller area. Next thing that you want to do is to make sure the spot is legal. Is it a tow away zone? Are there parking restrictions? Is there a fire hydrant next to the spot? Are you too close to the intersection? Once you find that ideal space, claim it, and prepare to park!

Park Your Car Like a Pro

On the following pages the skill of parallel parking will be broken up into five simple parts. Remember during each step, reference points are provided to make your parking experience more relaxed and stress-free. Understand however, as you become a more seasoned" parallel parker" you will be forced to make adjustments "on the fly" in order to finish with your car parked at that desired distance from the curb. Ideally a foot and one half or less away from the curb is preferred! Valuable adjustment tips will be provided for you later on in this book.

It is most important to learn the sequential steps first and learn to adjust later!

STEP 1

Find the ideal spot and claim it by turning on your right turn signal. Line up your side view mirror with the car you will be parking behind. Make sure your car is about three feet away from this car.

Coaching Point- Approach the vehicle you are parking behind slowly and make sure you are lined up parallel with it.

STEP 2

Crank your steering wheel all the way to the right (clockwise) shift to reverse, and roll back slowly until the back of your seat is lined up with the bumper of the other car. This position should create a forty five degree angle. This angle is the probably the most important part of the entire sequence.

Coaching Point- Always look back in the direction you are moving. Don't just rely on your rear view mirrors.

STEP 3

Now crank your wheel about one and one half rotations so that your wheels are totally straight. The steering wheel rotations may be a little more or a little less based on the vehicle you are driving. Usually between one rotation, and one and one half rotations of the steering wheel will do it. Continue to back up until your front bumper just passes the rear bumper of the car you are parking behind.

Coaching Point- Look back over your right shoulder as you continue in reverse.

STEP 4

As your bumper passes the rear bumper of the car you are parking behind, crank the wheel all the way to the left (counter clockwise). Roll back slowly until your car is parallel with the curb.

Coaching Point- As you become better at this skill you will know exactly how fast to move your hands when cranking the wheel. Practice makes perfect!

STEP 5

Finish the maneuver by shifting to drive, straightening your wheels and rolling forward toward the car you are parking behind.

Coaching Point- As you straighten your wheels try to move as slowly as possible so that you do not "undo" the critical turning radius that you have created with your steering wheel.

Step 1

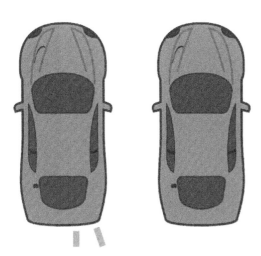

Signal Right as you approach the car you will be parking behind. Line up the side view mirror of your car with the side view mirror of the car you will be parking behind.

Step 2

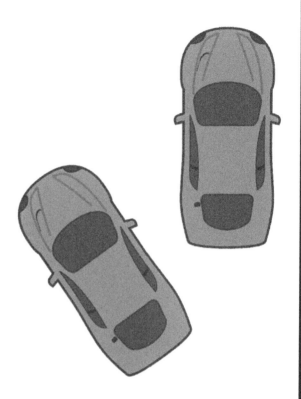

Crank your wheel all the way to the right (clockwise) and back up until you establish a 45 degree angle (your seat aligned with bumper).

Step 3

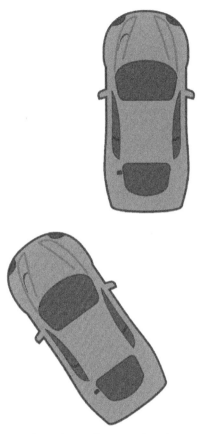

Straighten your wheel and continue to back up until your front end just passes the bumper of the car you are parking behind.

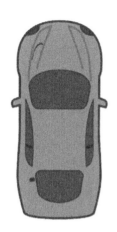

As your front end passes the bumper of the car you are parking behind crank the wheel hard to the left (counter clockwise).

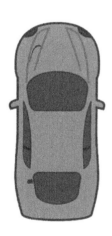

Step 5

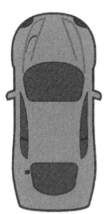

Complete the maneuver by straightening your wheel and rolling forward. Finish with your wheels straight.

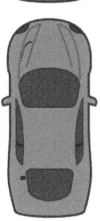

Make the Needed Adjustments

What makes this method so great is the fact that as you gain experience; simple adjustments can be adapted "on the fly" to make it even better. Learning how to identify when to adjust will become habit after many hours of practice.

While perfection may actually happen once and awhile, sometimes it will not, because of the following three factors:

1. The car you are parking behind is larger or smaller than the car you are parking behind.
2. The car you are parking behind is too far or too close to the curb.
3. The car you are parking behind is at an angle.

So what should we do? Remember this system is totally adjustable and adaptable. So with a couple of slight adjustments we can overcome these three problems and still park like a professional. The most important part of this system is the angle of entry (45 degrees). The angle of entry is when your car is at a forty five degree angle during step two of the system. This angle is critical because no matter how big or small the car you are parking behind it is still important to approach the curb at this forty five degree angle. That may mean backing up farther in step two or stopping earlier in step two. This becomes a learned habit after plenty of practice.

What if the car you are parking behind is too close or too far from the curb? Don't panic in order to adjust you have to either back up farther in step three or, simply crank into the parking spot a little bit sooner. Again this becomes a learned skill after plenty of practice.

If the car you are parking behind is angled try to adjust step one by lining up your vehicle with the curb itself, and then continue through the steps remembering that critical forty five degree angle of entry mentioned earlier.

LEAVE THE PARKING SPACE PROPERLY

Leaving a parallel parking space requires almost as much skill as parallel parking itself. Remember you are now exiting a very tight space with very little room to maneuver. When exiting a parking space you should:

1. Shift the car to reverse and back up slowly go back as far as you can without touching the car behind you. Remember to always look back in the direction you are moving.
2. Next shift to drive and crank the wheel all the way to the left (counter clockwise).

3. Signal left.
4. Check your mirrors.
5. Check your blind spot by physically looking over your left shoulder.
6. Roll forward slowly and move onto the road when traffic is clear.
7. Make sure that half of your car has passed the car you were parked behind before cranking to the right (clockwise).

CHAPTER 2 PARALLEL PARK METHOD B

The second method of parallel parking (Method B) requires less movement and in theory one less step than Method A. When it works you will look like a parallel parking professional; however when it doesn't, it can look somewhat embarrassing. The biggest difference between Method A and Method B is that in Method B you will have to back up more before cranking hard to the curb. This method is also commonly referred to as the "all or none method." It requires precision and accuracy and lots of on the road practice. This method does not allow for major adjustments "on the fly." Many experienced parallel parkers will graduate from Method A to Method B with continuous repetitions. Understanding angles of entry and proper steering wheel adjustments are critical when attempting to master Method B.

STEP 1
Start off by signaling right to let traffic know of your intention to parallel park. If the car is the same size as yours line up your side view mirrors approximately three feet away. If this car is larger than your car, attempt to line up the bumpers of each car. If it is smaller line up the

side view mirrors and be ready to make an adjustment on the fly.

Coaching Point- Make sure you are a minimum of three feet away from the car you will be parking behind! Any distance closer than that will not provide sufficient space to clear the car's bumper in front of you.

STEP 2

Crank the wheel all the way to the right (clockwise) and continue in reverse until your side view mirror is equal with the bumper of the car you will be parking behind. This angle formed with the other car should be at least 45 degrees (may be slightly larger angle since you are backing up farther).

Coaching Point- Stopping short and not creating a 45-50 degree angle will put you embarrassingly short of the curb. This system does not adjust well to a smaller angle! Sometimes you may even have to create a larger than 50 degree angle to get in close to the curb.

STEP 3

Now crank your wheel all the way to the left and roll back into position aligned with the car you are parking behind. Hopefully you will be within two feet of the curb.

Coaching Point- If you see that your angle is too small you may have to roll back straight before cranking hard toward the curb. If you feel your angle is too big then you may have to compensate by steering slightly left to lessen the angle.

STEP 4

Finish the maneuver by straightening your wheel and rolling slowly toward the car you are parking behind. Make sure your car wheels and steering wheel are straight.

Coaching Point- Make sure to crank hard toward the curb (clockwise) as you roll forward slowly. You do not want to "undo" the critical turning radius you have already created.

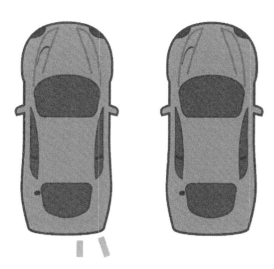

Signal Right as you approach the car you will be parking behind. Line up the side view mirror of your car with the side view mirror of the car you will be parking behind. If the cars are different lengths line up the rear bumpers of both cars.

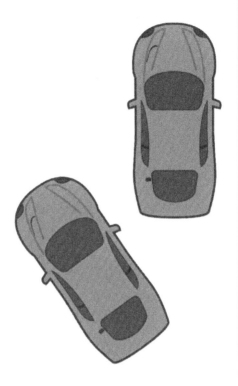

Crank your wheel all the way to the right
(clockwise) and back up until you establish a
45-50 degree angle (your side view mirror
aligned with bumper).

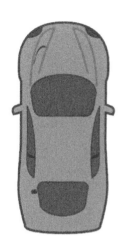

Now crank your wheel all the way to the left (counter clockwise) and roll back until you are aligned with the car you are parking behind..

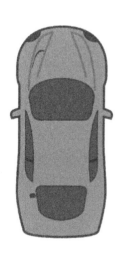

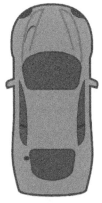

Complete the maneuver by straightening your wheel and rolling forward.

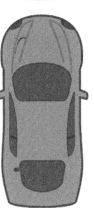

IT'S "ALL OR NONE"

As we stated before you can look like a pro when everything goes right in this system. Unfortunately adapting and adjusting to this system as a beginner can be a nightmare. In Method A every mistake you make can be adjusted for. Not the case with Method B. A small angle of entry will land you a lot further than the desired two feet or less from the curb. Important timely decisions must be well thought out as you approach your intended parking spot. Such things as how far away from the curb is the car you are parking behind must be considered. Also the length of the car that you will be parking behind must be swiftly calculated to ensure the proper angle of entry into the open parking space.

It is best advised as a newbie to start out, and master Method A first. Seasoned drivers with plenty of experience may want to tackle Method B because of its speed of entry. Whatever method you choose make sure to practice, practice, and more practice.

NEW DRIVERS

It is highly recommended that if you parallel park on your states' road test to use method A. The main reason the DMV assesses parallel parking on the road test is to see how you handle the car in reverse. Visual skills are of the utmost importance. Remember to look back whenever you shift to reverse. When you finish your parallel parking maneuver it is also important to signal, check your mirrors and check your blind spot before exiting the parking space.

CHAPTER 3 THREE POINT TURN

The three point turn sometimes referred to as the K turn is a simple change of direction maneuver. This maneuver is routinely tested on most state road examinations. It is a maneuver that will be used by all drivers at some time during their driving careers. The key to this maneuver is to perform it quickly and safely.

IS A THREE POINT TURN LEGAL?

Before performing any three point turn make sure that the turn is allowed. Are there any signs prohibiting the turn? Make sure you are on a two way road. Are there any signs indicating you may be on a one way road? Once you have decided that the turn is legal and necessary you can then prepare to perform the maneuver.

IS THERE ENOUGH CLEAR SPACE TO PERFORM A THREE POINT TURN?

The first step is to determine that you need to change direction and turn around. Next you must determine if the three point turn is legal. Finally you must determine if there is enough clear space to complete the maneuver. If the road is large enough to accommodate two vehicles side by side, chances are you will have enough space.

STEP 1

Signal right to indicate your intention to pull to the curb. You will want to pull as close to the curb as possible without hitting it.

Coaching Point- Make sure to pull close to that curb in order to help facilitate the maximum turning radius of your car.

STEP 2

Signal left to indicate your intention to perform a three point turn. Crank your wheel all the way to the left (counter clockwise) to achieve maximum turning radius. Be sure to check your side view mirror as well as your rearview mirror, and finish with a quick blind spot check over the left shoulder before rolling forward.

Coaching Point- Try to get as much cranking of the steering wheel finished before the car even begins to move.

STEP 3

Maintain the turning radius with your steering wheel and roll as far forward as possible without hitting the curb.

Coaching Point- Hold the wheel tight, maintain your turning radius as you roll to the curb.

STEP 4

Shift to reverse as you stop toward the opposite curb. Look back over your right shoulder as you crank the wheel all the way to the right (clock wise). Roll back as far as necessary without hitting the curb. Once you realize you have enough clear space to complete the maneuver you are done rolling backward.

Coaching Tip- Always shift the car first before you start cranking. Many inexperienced drivers forget to do this and continue to roll forward. This would be rather embarrassing on your driving road test.

STEP 5

Shift to drive and crank the steering wheel all the way to the left. Finish the maneuver by heading straight ahead, and by positioning your car in the opposite lane.

Coaching Tip- Again, do not forget to shift first! Once you have a sense that you can complete the turn easily, you are pretty much done backing up. This way you will not have to worry about hitting the curb, and the maneuver will proceed along more efficiently.

Signal Right and begin to move toward right curb.

Pull to the right curb and signal left. Crank your wheel all the way to the left, check your mirrors as well as your your left blind spot.

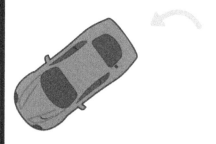

Keep the wheel all the way
cranked to the left, and roll to
the opposite curb as close as
possible without hitting it..

Shift to reverse and continue
to back up just befire hitting
the right curb.

Shift to drive, straighten the
wheel and complete the
maneuver.

FAST HANDS SLOW CAR!

Remember this mantra when performing any driving maneuver. "Fast hands" allow you to achieve a maximum turning radius quickly. "Slow car" allows you to use sound judgment concerning time and space when approaching the curb. You do not want to obstruct traffic flow, so make sure you complete the maneuver as fast and safe as possible. This may require some practice time.

NEW DRIVERS

The Three Point turn is one of the maneuvers tested on many State road tests, so be sure to adhere to the coaching points mentioned in the steps provided in this book. State examiners are not only gauging the efficiency of your three point turn, they are also watching your visual skills, and the overall judgement of your ability to handle the car in reverse. Hitting the curb could lose you valuable points on your road test. So as you approach the opposite curb, slow down and give yourself more time to judge that critical distance.

CHAPTER 4 PERPENDICULAR PARKING

Out of all of the driving maneuvers mentioned in this book, perpendicular parking will be the one that you will perform the most. Strip malls, hospitals and shopping centers to name a few all require precise perpendicular parking. Perpendicular parking requires proper steering, sound judgement of space size, and identification of a safe speed for your car. After all many "fender benders" occur in these large parking lots.

Perpendicular parking can be difficult because you will be asked to maneuver your car into a space as small as eight feet by fifteen feet, the relative size of a compact car. So it is important to keep your eyes moving and drive slowly in order to correctly identify the proper ninety degree parking angle. Below are the steps to help you perpendicular park properly and safely.

STEP 1
Signal left and maintain a minimum of eight feet of distance away from the parked cars or parking spaces on the left.

Coaching Point- Keep your eyes moving in order to identify any other cars exiting or entering nearby parking spaces. Proceed slowly and cautiously!

STEP 2
Begin to drift your car to the right in order to help achieve a maximum angle of entry.

Coaching Point- Identify early the left edge marking of the space you will be entering. Continue to scan the parking lot for other cars.

STEP 3
Begin your turn when you see the left edge marking of the parking space.

Coaching Point- Proceed slowly and keep the front end of your car "up and out" in preparation for a hard left turn.

STEP 4
Straighten your wheels as you complete the hard left turn and continue to center your car into the parking space.

Coaching Point- Finish with your wheels straight in order to assure an easy exit from the parking space.

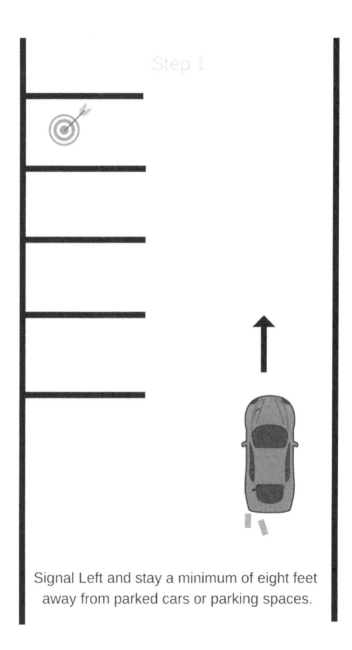

Signal Left and stay a minimum of eight feet
away from parked cars or parking spaces.

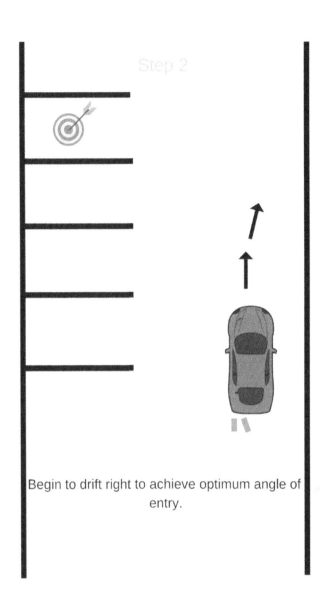

Begin to drift right to achieve optimum angle of entry.

Begin to turn when you can see the left edge marking of parking space.

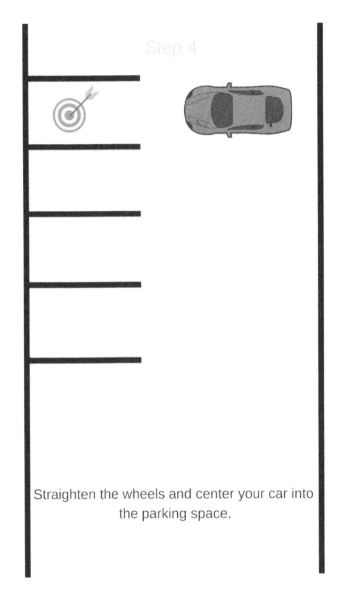

Straighten the wheels and center your car into the parking space.

EXITING THE PARKING SPACE

Exiting a perpendicular space can be as equally if sometimes more dangerous than entering the space. Turn on your signal and flash your break lights to warn other cars of your intentions to leave the space. Back up slowly, scanning over your shoulder. Look right and left as you continue to back up. When more than half your car has exited the space begin to crank your steering wheel in the direction you plan to travel. Make sure your front fender clears the car you are parked alongside .As your car enters the lane of traffic begin to straighten your wheel and shift to drive. Exit the parking lot slowly and cautiously while continuing to scan for entering and exiting cars.

HANDLING A RIGHT SIDE PARKING SPACE
Handling a parking spot on the right side is done exactly the same way as the left side. The main difference is that now you will be signaling right, and drifting to the left side of the traffic lane. The right edge marking will now become your reference point when positioning your car into the space.

BACKING INTO A PERPENDICULAR SPOT
Many experienced drivers prefer to back into a perpendicular spot. This may be advantageous since it allows for a quicker and safer exit from

the spot. Using the same technique of "drifting" to the opposite side of the traffic lane, and identifying the edge marking of space or car requires a lot of confidence and practice. New drivers may want to practice with cones or in an empty parking lot before trying this in a crowded mall parking lot.

Chapter 5 Two Point Turns

The most skilled drivers will ultimately make a mistake at some time during their driving lifetime. Missing a turn, street or building will definitely happen at some point during your driving career. Many times a two point turn becomes a better and safer option when looking to perform a turnabout. This chapter will show two of the easiest most common methods on how to perform a two point turn.

Backing into a Driveway

Once you have determined that you have passed your intended destination it is time to prepare for the execution of a two point turn. As with any change of direction maneuver make sure there are no signs prohibiting this turnabout. It is also a great idea to have maximum visibility, which means no hills or curves that obstruct your line of sight. Remember to be patient if there is heavy traffic, and always watch out for pedestrians and cyclists. (Diagram A)

Step 1
Locate the driveway or alleyway you plan to use for your turn and pull past it.

Coaching Point- Make sure the driveway or alleyway is unobstructed and wide enough to accommodate your vehicle.

STEP 2

Signal right and pull to about three feet from the curb. Shift into reverse and check for any obstacles in your intended path.

Coaching Point- Make sure there is plenty of clear space in front and behind you. Check your rear view mirror and remember to look back over your right shoulder as you go in reverse.

STEP 3

Turn your wheel sharply to the right as you continue to look over your right shoulder. Begin to straighten your wheels by turning your steering wheel to the left. Back up until your car is straight and has cleared the roadway or curb.

Coaching Point- Use the right edge of the driveway or alleyway as a key reference point when driving in reverse.

STEP 4

Shift to drive and signal left. Check traffic in both directions. Pull out and straighten your wheels to complete the maneuver.

Coaching Point- Make sure there is plenty of clear space to the right and left sides of the road before exiting the driveway.

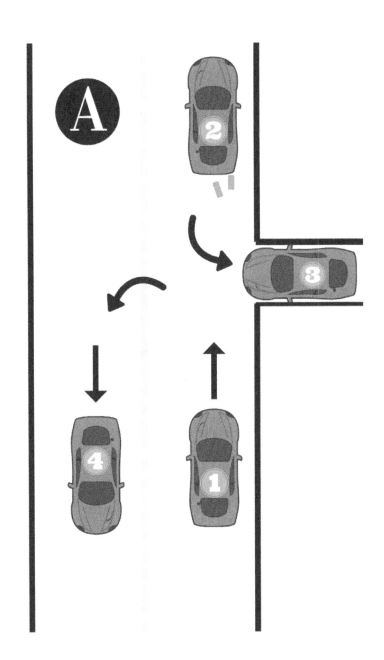

PULLING INTO A DRIVEWAY

The second method of two point turning involves using a driveway or alleyway on the left side of the road. The most difficult part of this maneuver will be backing up onto the street itself. (Diagram B)

STEP 1

Signals left and pull into an unobstructed driveway or alleyway on the left side of the road.

Coaching Point- Make sure to give motorists behind you plenty of warning by signaling your intent to turn early. Check for other cars and pedestrians before completing your turn.

STEP 2

Shift to reverse and begin to back up slowly. Make sure to look over your right shoulder as you back up.

Coaching Point- Use the right edge of the roadway as your reference point as you back onto the roadway.

STEP 3

Make sure to crank the wheel all the way to the right (clock wise) as you back up into the roadway. Once you are on the road begin to turn your steering wheel left to straighten your car.

Coaching Point- Continue to look back over your right shoulder until your car is centered in the roadway.

STEP 4

Shift to drive and continue to straighten your steering wheel has you head down the road.

Coaching Point- Make one more important check for any obstacles or pedestrians before you accelerate forward.

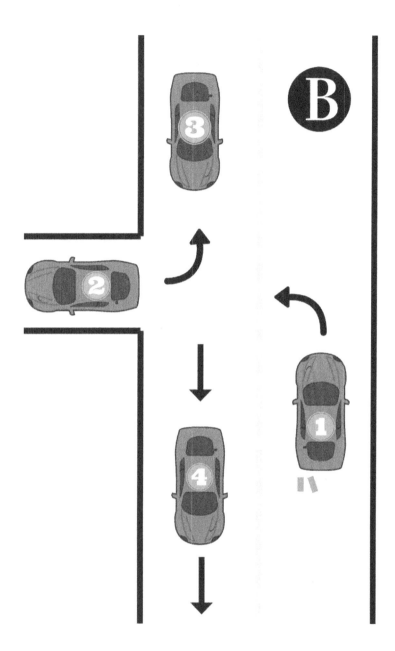

Chapter 6 Parking on a Grade

Believe it or not there is a technique for parking on an uphill or downhill grade. It is imperative that your car not have the ability to roll into traffic after you lock it up and leave it. In this chapter procedures for parking on a roadway with an uphill and downhill grade will be presented. These procedures will be presented with both a curb and without a curb.

Parking Uphill With a Curb

Step 1
Begin by parking your car parallel to the curb

Step 2
As you move forward turn your wheels sharply to the left.

Step 3
Shift your car to neutral and with your foot on the brake roll back slowly until your right front tires touch the curb. Set your parking brake. If you have a manual transmission, shift to first gear.

PARKING UPHILL WITHOUT A CURB

STEP 1

Begin by parking your car parallel with the side of the road.

STEP 2

As you move forward turn your wheels sharply to the right.

STEP 3

Set your parking brake. If the car does begin to roll it will roll safely off the roadway.

Parking on an
Uphill Grade with
a Curb

Without a
Curb

PARKING ON A DOWNHILL GRADE WITH A CURB

STEP 1
Park your car in a position parallel with the curb. Turn the steering wheel sharply right and roll forward slowly until your right front tire touches the curb.

STEP 2
Before you lock your doors and walk away, set your parking brake. If you have a manual transmission shift the car in reverse.

PARKING ON A DOWNHILL WITHOUT A CURB

STEP 1
Park your car parallel to the shoulder as close to the shoulder as possible. Turn your steering wheel sharply right again as close to the shoulder as possible.

STEP 2
Set your parking brake. If you have a manual transmission, shift your car into reverse.

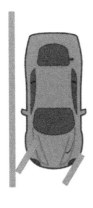

Parking on a
Downhill
Grade with a
Curb

Without a
Curb

CHAPTER 7 PREPARING FOR THE ROAD TEST

Passing your road test and getting your drivers' license is one of the most rewarding and exciting periods in a young person's life. It can also be very stressful if you are not properly prepared. Every state is different in their handling of the final evaluation of driving skill. Some states require an examination of driving ability in traffic, while others may conduct their testing on a closed course. It is important to understand what skills will be emphasized on your own state's exam.

If you followed and completed all the lessons in this book and practiced them, you will be more than adequately prepared to pass the maneuvers portion of your road test. In this section you will be provided with some final critical advice, so that you will be able to pass your test with flying colors.

TAKE CARE OF YOUR BODY

Get a good night's sleep and eat properly the day before your test. You need to be alert and ready to go when you arrive at the road test site. It is a good idea to mentally rehearse all the skills that you have learned in preparation for this big event. The visual skills and habits need to be automatic on this day. Remember the visual pattern of signal, mirror, and blind spot. This visual sequence will be evaluated several times on your exam. Leaving the curb at the start of the test, changing lanes, three point turns and exiting your parallel park are just a few of times that this important skill will be tested.

SECURE YOUR PAPERWORK

Most states require that you have your permit as well as proof of completion of a pre-licensing class, which is also required by many states before taking your road test. Make sure that your vehicle has been inspected, and that you have copies of both your insurance documents as well as the cars registration papers. Check out your states drivers' manual in order to determine which documents are required. Also have a personal check ready in case you need to pay for any licensing fees right there on the spot.

PREPARE YOUR CAR

A clean vehicle is a signal to the road test examiner that you are a disciplined mature driver. It is a good idea to vacuum and clean the vehicle before your road test. Clean the windows and mirrors throughout the car for maximum visibility. Check the fuel level and clean the headlights. Make sure mechanically that your car is ready to go. Do a final check of all systems before heading out. The last thing you want to happen is to have your car "stall" during the middle of your exam. A clean well performing vehicle is a reflection of your driving personality. Make sure you make a good first impression.

TEST DAY

The day has finally arrived and so has your stress level. Relax take a deep breath and rest assured that if you have practiced and prepared, you are more than ready to nail this thing. Wait patiently for the road test examiner to arrive. Make sure your seat and head rests are adjusted properly. Check your mirrors and make sure they are positioned for maximum visibility. Put your seat belt on and make sure you turn off any distractions such as cell phones and the radio. Make sure you have all the necessary paperwork.

When the examiner arrives hand them the paperwork and remain positive at all times. Let them do the talking and concentrate heavily on every direction that they give you. It's ok to admit you are nervous, but remember once the exam begins, be confident and let your practice preparation take over. Never admit a mistake, and if you do make one do not dwell on it. The examiner will be taking notes both positive and negative, do not obsess over this. It is their job to file a report on each and every exam they administer.

Once the exam is completed show respect to the examiner by thanking them. Many states now have interactive exams and share the results with you immediately. Some will even go over the entire test with you. If you do pass, congratulations on a job well done. If you do not, be sure to find out what you did wrong, so that you can practice for it, and be ready the next time.

Understand that once you do receive your driver's license that it is only the beginning. Driving is an ongoing process and you will continue to learn each and every day. There is no substitute for experience. Matter of fact, one in three new drivers will be involved in a collision or receive at ticket in their first year of driving. In order to stay collision free, remember to drive defensively each and every day, and use the skills and strategies that this book has laid out for you.

CHECKLIST OF SKILLS FOR THE ROAD TEST
Here is a list of skills that most states require you to perform on your road test. Make sure you

practice them over and over until they become habit.

1. Speed: Make sure you stay at or below the speed limit for the road test area. Be aware of any school zones.
2. Braking: Smooth gradual braking. Make sure you make complete stops (no rolling) at all stop signs. Failure to make a complete stop will result in an automatic failure.
3. Lateral Maneuvers: Make sure to signal, check your mirrors and check your blind spot in that order every time, on each and every lateral maneuver. This includes leaving the curb as well as lane changes.
4. Following Distance: Make sure to maintain a minimum two second following distance behind other vehicles for speeds under 45mph.
5. Right of Way Laws: Make sure you follow right of way laws to a tee! Four way stops and left hand turns are two examples that you may be confronted with on the road test. At a four way stop, remember the car that arrives first, goes first. If two cars arrive at the same time then the car on the right goes first. When making a left hand

turn remember to keep your wheels straight, and if the light turns red, you have the right to complete your turn when traffic allows.

6. Signal: Communicate all of your maneuvers and turns by signaling early.

7. Three Point Turn or K Turn: Make sure you have this skill down to a science. Remember to signal away from curb, and to always look in the direction you are moving.

8. Parallel Parking: Once again practice this skill until you are confident that you will be able to perform it with skill time after time. Look back over the shoulder when going in reverse and don't forget to signal.

9. Backing Up: Remember to always look in the direction you are moving until you come to a stop. Some states require that you back up into a parking spot on your road exam.

10. Turning: Remember to keep the front end of the car out and stay in your lane when making right and left hand turns. The rear wheels do not track the same way as your front wheels. Use proper hand over hand turning and

accelerate smoothly through all of your turns.

Good luck and always remember that practice and proper preparation are the keys to passing the road test. Also remember that passing the road test is only the beginning of your journey. Drive safely and defensively every time you get behind the wheel. Immaturity and lack of experience are the main reasons for the high incidence of new driver collisions. Handling a 2000 pound vehicle is no easy task. Please take this task very seriously. Eighty percent of all accidents on our road ways are preventable. Make it your personal mission to make each and every road and highway a safer place all across this nation!

CHAPTER 8 OTHER BOOKS AND WEBSITE INFORMATION

You can get plenty of free information regarding all topics in the field of driver education by going to www.driveredcoach.com. On this website you can find valuable information on the latest driving techniques as well as important information to help you pass your road test.

I hope you found this book to be a valuable resource in your quest to secure a driver's license or just help you to perform simple driving maneuvers. Hopefully the information you learned will carry over onto the state roads and highways. My intention in writing this book was not only to help you pass the road test portion of the licensing procedure, but also to help you learn the skills necessary in order to help you navigate the Highway Transportation System safely and successfully. It is also important for you to establish a critical partnership with your parents or guardians when setting up your practice driving sessions. I would strongly recommend that you seek out professional driving lessons either in a certified driver education program or through lessons with a private driving school. It will also be equally important for your parents or guardians to seek out the latest information regarding proper driving techniques and defensive driving skills. I have a couple of these books listed at the end of this chapter for a relatively low cost. .After all of these skills have been taught, and you feel you have reached a mastery level of knowledge, these critical skills you have learned must always continue to be reinforced throughout your driving lifetime.

As a way of expressing my thanks for your purchase, I am offering a FREE Guide to help you pass your road test. Just go to www.driveredcoach.com to claim your FREE Guide. Add your email to get special offers and updates on future publications and courses.

RECOMMENDED BOOKS TO HELP YOU LEARN HOW TO DRIVE THE CORRECT WAY:
"Teach Your Teenager How to Drive a Car" Sequential Lessons for a New Driver

"Save Your Teenage Driver's Life" Important Strategies to Teach a New Driver Now!

THANK YOU
I hope you found "this book helpful and will continue to use this as an important resource regarding appreciate you leaving a short honest review on the Amazon Kindle website. This

feedback will allow me to continue writing Kindle books that produce positive life changing results. Thanks again for purchasing and reading my book. Keep an eye out for future titles in the Driver and Traffic Safety field as well as several titles in the Health, Fitness and Wellness fields.

Made in the USA
Las Vegas, NV
18 December 2024